Reserve or Renew Online
at
www.pbjclibrary.org/catalog

D0285645

300 Anderson
White Hall, AR 71602

Food for the Power of Thinking, Book II

DATE DUE

GAYLORD — PRINTED IN U.S.A.

Food for the Power of Thinking, Book II

The Roots of the Races

by

Rev. Dr. Antony O. Hobbs, Sr., Ed.D.

White Hall Library
300 Anderson
White Hall, AR 71602

DORRANCE PUBLISHING CO., INC.
PITTSBURGH, PENNSYLVANIA 15222

All Rights Reserved
Copyright © 2007 by Rev. Dr. Antony O. Hobbs, Sr., Ed.D.
No part of this book may be reproduced or transmitted
in any form or by any means, electronic or mechanical,
including photocopying, recording, or by any information
storage and retrieval system without permission in
writing from the publisher.

ISBN: 978-0-8059-7503-1
Library of Congress Control Number: 2006934756
Printed in the United States of America

First Printing

For more information or to order additional books, please contact:
Dorrance Publishing Co., Inc.
701 Smithfield Street
Third Floor
Pittsburgh, Pennsylvania 15222
U.S.A.
1-800-788-7654
www.dorrancebookstore.com

Dedication

This work is dedicated to my beloved wife, Letha May; my five children: Bonita R., Antony O. Jr., Carolyn R., Walter E., and Marshall K., and all who seek truth.

Contents

Foreword

As a relatively young black woman nearing my fortieth birthday, I find myself asking these questions. Is there more to "our" story than we've been told? What is this silent but pervasive "thing" that is keeping us, as a race, "shackled" to our circumstances? Why aren't we moving forward—why can't we? Why are we unable or unwilling to love ourselves and our brothers and sisters enough to lift each other as *we* climb? Are "they" holding us back, or are we holding ourselves back, stunting our own growth?

We as a race have been tremendously blessed and favored of God to have been persecuted, yet have persevered—to have suffered trials, yet we have triumphed—to have been battered but not broken. God has, indeed, brought us from a mighty long way! Yet many of my peers seem to be bound by a sort of "slave mentality," and we are not of the generation of those who were actually enslaved!

I must admit that it was not until I reached my early thirties that I was even aware of the undercurrent of racism that was so cleverly hidden under the disguise of working in the "good" jobs with the "good" white people who allowed me to associate with them at their luncheons and office Christmas parties, to let me sit at the front desk and smile "pretty" and dress up nice, and to show the world they had no problem with "us." But when promotion time came and raises were discussed, my evaluations never quite met their standards, even though I worked myself to a frazzle, doing the most menial duties they could find for me to do without complaint, and of course, being expected to smile all while I was cleaning the grass stains from the shoes of the "good" white boss, taking his shirts to the cleaners, or washing everyone's coffee cups two or three times a day. "You just need to smile more." "Get more involved and innovative with your work." "Don't complain." "No one is irreplaceable." In other words, stay in your "place."

It was a bitter pill to swallow, but it made me stronger, as trials are meant to do. It also opened my eyes to some very real issues that are going unnoticed and unchallenged in our society, and I fear that if more of our people don't open their eyes—and soon—we will have an opportunity to experience firsthand what the slave mentality is really about.

I met Dr. Hobbs in October of 2000, when the Lord sent him to shepherd the flock at the church I attended in Arkadelphia, Arkansas. I knew from the first instant he spoke that he was no simple preachin' man. He immediately started addressing the questions and issues that had been plaguing my mind. His vast research and knowledge of the roots of our race amazed and strengthened me—intellectually, emotionally, spiritually, and ethnically.

He opened up a whole new vista of awareness of who we really are and why we have a right to love ourselves—God-given right. His platform was not focused on hatred of the white man but rather on understanding who we are and loving ourselves enough to know that we *do* deserve to be called *Children of God*, that we have right to own our own businesses, to take charge of our own economic condition, and to be educated in the full knowledge of who and *whose* we are.

I am proud to have met the author of this book and to have had him as a mentor in my life even for such a short time. To God be the Glory!

Krishna Davis, a Friend

Acknowledgements

The preparation of this work required the participation and cooperation of many individuals and diverse groups. How each one assisted in the completion of this book would require an additional chapter.

I, however, acknowledge with great appreciation the inspiration and encouragement provided by my give children: Bonita, Antony Jr., Carolyn ElVisto, Walter, and Marshall, who were constant sources of help in the completion of this work.

I wish to express my appreciation to Tamara Earls of Humphrey, Arkansas, for the typing of the draft copy.

And finally, my sincere thanks to Marcia Burns of Jacksonville, Arkansas, who was a constant source of assistance in the completion of this book.

Introduction

Dear reader, you might feel that at times during this work, I have written with a big of anger. That is because I was angry. You see, this work and research was done over a period of four decades.

In concluding this work in 1999, at a time when much of society had changed, I thought of rewriting those passages that showed my anger; however, after giving thought to the purpose of this book, I decided not to change that part that showed anger of the racist times in which it was written. I am thankful to God to say that I am not angry today because of the progress that has been made in race relations over the past thirty years. This does not say that things are equal, as they should be, but they are so much better than they were thirty years ago.

The objective of this book is to trace the origin of the races, showing that the first people of creation were people of color—black, brown, and other shades of complexions, but not white. It is to show the black nations of the Holy Bible and their disbursement worldwide. It is to inform, motivate, and educate African and African-American pastors and laymen to the importance of Africans and African-Americans, knowing ancient African history as well as contemporary history of black achievements in America and the world.

Please note that we are the only ethnic group on earth who has such poor understanding of our history. If you do not know your history, you do not know who you are. Thus, you cannot respect yourself and those who look like you; therefore, it is impossible for other races to respect you as you would like to be.

Please note that knowing one's history gives one a kind of pride that commands respect for another. Thus, we can truly "love one another."

The objective of this work is to labor to trace the descendants of Ham, the father of the "black race," for the purpose of informing the present-day Hamites of their world history and to show where they were and are presently located on the world scene. Also, it will open the eyes of the descendants of Japheth (white race) to the oversight on the part of many white scholars of today. This was due to a deliberate conspiracy conceived by colonial Americans for the purpose of putting to shame and misinforming all people of African (Hamite) descent and persuading the well-meaning white people (Japhites) to believe Africans were naturally inferior to them.

Thus, the black pastors must envision their mission of discipleship in this new century as the key toward reeducating black people out of Eurocentric mental and spiritual incarceration by first learning where African nations are in the Holy Bible. They must also learn the positive roles the nations have played in world civilization and teach this to their congregations.

Pastors, by doing this, you will be making a giant step toward doing God's will, which is placing Africans in a first-class citizenship position worldwide. Will you please help me get this message out to our people?

Introduction of Terms

Ham refers to all people of color, particularly those of very dark hue. The reason for this, using the story of the Great Flood found in Genesis, was that all people were derived from Noah and his three sons: Ham, Shem, and Japheth. Japheth was the progenitor of what became the white race many centuries later. Ham and Shem were both what westerners would classify as black.

I feel there is no way to distinguish Hamites from Shemites because history shows the two groups lived and interacted through marriage down through the centuries.

Japheth (white) was the progenitor of the Europeans and their descendants, also called western civilization (white civilization).

In this work, the terms Hamite, black, and negroes will be used to describe the same people.

Chapter 1

The Color or Complexion of Adam and Eve (Parents of the Human Race) and All People before the Flood, Including the Hebrews

In order to ascertain the information that will lead us to the knowledge of the complexion of Adam and Eve, the parents of the present human race, I shall refer first to a very ancient and learned historian, Flavius Josephus. Josephus states in his work, *Antiquities of the Jews, Book 1*, page twelve, that "Adam, the first man, according to the Bible, was created red or dark. God took dust from the ground and formed man. He inserted in him a spirit and a soul. This man was called Adam, which in the Hebrew language means 'one who is red or dark, because he was formed of dark earth, compounded together, for that kind is virgin or true earth.'" It is written by Moses in Genesis 5:2 that God called the first parents of this human race by but one name, which was that of Adam, in which name was understood as well as their natures and their complexion.

God did not give the first woman the name Eve. It was Adam who did this when he understood that she was to become the mother of the human race. "Adam" was the name God gave to the man as well as to the woman at first. This is shown in Genesis 5:2. In Genesis it is written, "Male and female he created, and blessed them, and called their names Adam in the day when they were created."

In accordance with this statement of Josephus, in giving a reason why God called the first two human beings by one name and that name being Adam, or the dark man and woman, I find the Hebrew language establishes that the words

1

"Adam," "Adamah," and "Adami" all have a similar meaning. (1) Adam signifies earthly man, dark. (2) Adamah signifies dark earth or blood. (3) Adami signifies earthly dark red or blood. All of these names are of the same class and spring from the same root, which was Adam, meaning red or copper color, dark.

From a view of the above facts, it should be difficult to account for the reasons of the name of the first man or woman, unless they were created dark in color instead of white. As it is well known, the Hebrew language is governed in its power by naming *visible existence* as animals, fowls, fish, etc., by their appearance or nature and frequently by both as in the case of the name "Adam," which not only represented the hue of the skin, but that also of his intellectual existence or human nature.

Complexion of People before the Flood

The Jewish historians, as well as the Hebrew language, furnished us with clues leading to the right conclusion on the subject that Adam and all the people before the Great Flood were people of color, not white, since they were dark red or black.

Additional information on this subject is evident in the writing of Moses in the book of Genesis, Chapters 5 and 7, as well as in a narrative of the births and deaths of the patriarchs from the beginning to the time they lived, a lapse of about 2533 years and about 1481 years before the birth of Josephus, the Hebrew historian. This is evidence in relation to the belief that Adam was created colored. Thus, dark color is given by Moses in tracing the genealogical descent of one of the sons of Adam—that of Seth, from his father down to the patriarch, Jacob, who was the immediate progenitor of the twelve tribes of the house of Israel.

Seth, being one of the sons of Adam and Eve, was the direct progenitor of the Hebrew or Jewish people, commonly called the Holy Seed. The genealogy of that race is traced down from Adam to Noah, then from Abraham to Jacob, the father of the twelve tribes of Israel (Genesis, Chapters 5, 6, 21, 25 and 35).

From Seth to Jacob

I am giving an extract from chapters of the book of Genesis—5, 11, 21, and 35—respecting this genealogy as follows: Seth, the son of Adam, was the father of Enos, who was the father of Cainan, who was the father of Mahalaleel, who was the father of Jared, who was the father of Enoch, who was the father of Methuselah, who was the father of Lamech, who was the father of Noah, who was the father of Shem, who was the father of Arpahad, who was the father of Salah, who was the father of Eber, who was the father of Noah, who was the father of Reu, who was the father of Serug, who was the father of Noah, who was the father of Terah, who was the father of Abraham, who was the father of Isaac, who was the father of Jacob, who was the father of the Jews or of Israel. It is well known by historians of antiquity that the Jews of old, or pure Jews, were people of color, colored, dark, and not white as many appear today. Thus, I have shown with the father of the human race, Adam, that the first people were of color, not white. I will explain in later work the reason for the present-day "White Jews."

Summary

Finally, from the facts established, I believe it is clear that the complexion of Adam, Eve, and the people before the flood were not white, but people of color, dark. Due to the practice of racism for the past several hundred years, many persons have been led to believe that God created the first people white and their descendants have, in many cases and countries, been changed into the hues and complexions by the actions of the elements. That is not the truth. Should it be true that the first people were white, Adam would not have been called Adam, meaning "man of color."

Should the reader wish to know why I have followed the line of genealogy of Seth, the third son of Adam, when the scriptures speak of two other sons and many daughters, why select Seth in preference to all the others? The reason is that the descendants of all the other sons were lost in the flood. There was, therefore, no other genealogy to trace, meaning there was only Noah's genealogy.

I wish to state again that due to white racism over the past several hundred years, many people in Christian countries have been misinformed, thus believing that Adam, Eve, and the first people on earth were white. This includes the Jews, the prophets, and patriarchs of the Bible. None of the Bible patriarchs of the Old Testament were of the white race.

Let us move into the new age and learn the truth. According to John 8:32, "the truth will set you free." As you read the following chapter, this truth will be revealed.

The complexion of the first parents, Adam and Eve, was of dark hue. This truth has been covered up for most by a few. Why did they do this? To give themselves more power and might? Thanks be to God in the fulfillment of this time he brings the truth to light. And his truth revealed in the Holy Bible shows Adam and Eve could not have been white.

And the truth of God cuts sharper than a two-edged sword, but it is always right. In the twenty-first century, God's people will face this truth and will not fight, and in a few decades, color racism will disappear from the world's sight.

Chapter 2

Could Other Races and Complexions Have Been Produced by Climate and/or Locations?

In chapter one, I hope to have established sufficient facts to cause the reader to believe that all people before the Great Flood were people of color, or dark. Now the causes of different races and complexions are raised. How did there become other races with different complexions, such as extreme black and extreme white, varying from the original people of color? The central questions then is could the races and complexions have been produced by climate or location of persons on earth?

After a close investigation and examination of facts concerning the central question, my argument would be that the coldest regions of the earth have not changed the color of the skin, formation of the body and limbs, or type of hair on the head of the different races, although climate has caused temporary change in the shades of complexions. For example, in extreme heat, one becomes a little darker, and in extremely cold climates, where there is little sun, one becomes temporarily lighter in complexion. The race of the persons, however, remains the same in body formation and hair texture. For example, the African blacks have dwelt for many years in cold regions of the earth, yet they are black people still with their peculiar formation of body and hair. There has been no effective material change by any such cause. The same is equally true as it relates to the white race, who lived in the hot parts of the world.

Doctrine of Climate As Cause to Produce Different Races Refuted

In proof of this doctrine, the changeless character of the races, we will note that on the eastern coast of Africa, black (copper-colored) and white inhabitants have been found. The whites found in those regions are supposed to be the descendants of the ancient Romans from around 100 B.C.

This fact, that of white inhabitants being found in this black country, Africa, is stated by John Leo, who wrote a history of ancient Africa in the Arabic language entitled *Morse Uni Feo*, vol. 2, pp. 754–781.

Procopius, a Greek historian of the sixth century, speaks of a race of fair complexion with yellow hair who lived in the Libyan part of North Africa, south and west of ancient Egypt, and who was likely of Greek and Roman origin also.

The same people were found by Dr. Thomas Shaw, the Antiquarian who wrote in the seventeenth century and stated that they retained their fair complexions and yellow hair over a lapse of more than a thousand years from the time of Procopius and that of Dr. Shaw (Amer. Encyclopedia vol. 8, past p. 688) in Abyssinia, which is a region of Africa. In the *Universal Travel*, p. 467, it says, "There are found a population of many tribes of various colors, as black, copper color, and white or nearly so." How is this? Why does not the climate make them all black alike, if the black of the "negro" is the work of climate alone? It is because the opinion that climate determines race is false.

Reverend Michael Russell, L.L.D., author of *View of Ancient and Modern Egypt, Palestine of the Holy Land*, stated that in regards to the people of Ethiopia (Abyssinia), who are now and have been for more than 2,300 years mixed with Arabs (Shem and Ham mixture), a dark, copper-colored race, and though by their language, it is impossible to distinguish one from the other. Yet by their physiological qualities in features and form, they are easily distinguished from the Arabs, thus the power is in the "blood" of the races.

On the subject of climate causing races, I shall conclude with statements from the popular lecture of physiology by Professor Lawrence, who maintains that the longest series of ages is found incapable of changing the races, whatever the climate may be (Lawrence lectures, p. 257).

This being true of which we should not doubt, it has been shown and even demonstrated that at some ancient time period, the color white must have had its own origin without owing it to the influence of climate and was radically fixed by some competent power, (GOD) in the "blood" of the races.

The Origin of the Black and White Races and Proof That Ham Was Black

Dear reader, please keep in mind that at this point in time, there were only two races or classifications of humans: the dark (original humans, or "black") and the white. Now, if these two complexions of the human race were not produced by climate or by other natural circumstances, thus the central question of this chapter is:

How then were they produced? In relation to the dark (first humans), I have already shown the origin, which was given by God to Adam in his creation.

In this chapter, I shall show how the whites had their beginning. It is known even to the elementary student of the Holy Bible in the book of Genesis that Noah fathered three sons before the Great Flood and these three sons were named Shem, Ham, and Japheth. I have defined Ham and Shem as being the same origin as their parents, Noah and his wife; thus, this complexion was dark.

According to Josiah Priest, author of *American Antiquities* and member of the Antiquarian Society of New York, the following is how the white race came into being. He said that God, who made all things and endowed all animated nature with the strange and unexplained power of propagation, superintended the formation of this son of Noah in the womb of his mother in an extraordinary and supernatural manner, giving to this child such form of body, constitutions of nature and complexions of skin, as suited his will. This son was Japheth, whom God caused to be born white or fair, differing from the color of his parents, who were dark, while God caused Ham and Shem to be born dark, a complexion different from Japheth. Thus, Priest goes on to say that it was therefore by the miraculous intervention of the divine power that the white man had been produced equally as much as the creation of the color of the first man, Adam, the creator giving him a complexion that pleased The Divine Will.

In a later work, I will give the reason for God causing them (the new races) to be created. At this time, however, I will continue in my labor to give proof of the complexion of the father of the "black race." Ham was dark, and since the reader may not be as well satisfied as I am that in the above described manner the black race had its origin, I shall present other evidence of the alleged fact.

The circumstance to which I now allude is the name that was given to the black son of Noah at his birth. Keep in mind that in the language of Noah, as well as in the same language that was later called Hebrew, in naming persons and things, this was descriptive of the person or thing named.

So the word "Ham," in the language of Noah, which was the purest and most ancient Hebrew, signified anything that was black or dark.

Please note that scholars of theology acknowledge that the true Antediluvian, Adamic, or Hebrew language acknowledges the language spoke by Noah. The language of Adam was continued in the line of Seth, which is termed the Holy Seed of the Patriarchs down to Noah, and from Noah to Jacob, the father of the "Jews." Unless what I have written was the fact, it would be impossible, I believe, to ascertain the record of history of the creation—the manner of the Antediluvian, the names and ages of the patriarch, in the line of Seth down to Noah and the deeds and acts of many persons who lived before the deluge. And then they were being transmitted to all ages and nations since the Great Flood. I believe the accounts now alluded to were not delivered to Moses by direct inspiration. This is shown by there having been knowledge of these things in the family of Noah, and of course, among the descendants of his house, from the time of the flood down to Abraham and from there to Moses. He only wrote news from old written records and spoken accounts, a history of facts brought down from beyond the flood by the lineage of Seth to Adam written in Adamic language.

Information of all these things possessed by Noah and the succeeding patriarchs of the line of Shem, Ham, and Japheth—the sons of Noah—is evident from Moses' own account, as he refers to the fact of Noah's children. And the patriarchs, even down to Abraham and Melchisedec, understood the will of God and the history of past ages, as referred to by Moses' own accounts in his book of Genesis. Consequently, God could not have just made them known to him by *divine inspiration* as he wrote the books. The whole book of Genesis is full of reference to the knowledge of the ancient, especially of the line of Seth, Noah, Abraham, Melchisedec, and other patriarchs before this time.

Thus the "white" race came into being by the miraculous intervention of God.

Climate and Location Cannot Produce a Race

The coldest or hottest regions of the earth have never produced a race of man, not even a tribe or clan, although climate can change one from light to tan. But color is but one small aspect of the race of man.

There were physiological qualities in features and form that distinguish Ham, Japheth, and Shem.

Chapter 3

Modern Ethiopia

The Capital of Ethiopia is Addis Ababa. The official language is Amharic. The population, estimated in 1984, is 47,709,000. The chief products of agriculture are coffee, corn, oil seed, sorghum, sugar cane, tiff, and wheat; manufacturing products are cement, processed food, shoes, and textiles. Among Africa's nations, only Nigeria and Egypt have more people.

Ethiopian Religion

As many as 40 percent of Ethiopia's people belonged to the Ethiopian Orthodox Church, a Christian faith. About 40 percent of the people are Muslims and 20 percent Beta Israelites, a form of Judaism. They are sometimes called black Jews because they have dark skin.

The language spoken by the Ethiopians (Amharic) was a "Semitic" language of the same classification of that which King Solomon spoke. This language is the language of Noah, thus in early history, the language of his sons, Ham (the black man), Japheth (the white man), and Shem (the copper- or dark-colored man).

Dear reader, I think at this time it is proper and fitting that I bring out how the term "Shamite," or "Shemitic language," has been used by historians and scholars in a misleading way. Their misuse of the word has caused many readers to believe that all of those ancient civilizations who spoke the Shemitic language were Hebrews or Jews. This is not true; however, in order for one to understand what I am saying, one would need to have knowledge of the origin of the term "Shamite," or "Shemitic language," as I shall give below.

History and Origin of the Word "Shemitic"

The word "Shemitic" is derived from Shem, one of the sons of Noah, who was the progenitor or forefather of Abraham of the Bible, thus the father of the Israelites. Through Shem's lineage, the "word of God" has been given to the world. "Shemitic" is an adjective describing the language and culture of Shem. His generations, however, were not the only people of the ancient world who spoke the "Shemitic tongue," inasmuch as this language was the language of Shem's father, Noah. Noah's other two sons, Ham (the black son) and Japheth (the white son), also spoke the same tongue as their father, Noah, and brother Shem. Now, dear reader, with the knowledge of the origin of the term "Shemitic," as I have stated above, I feel that you will agree with me when I state that historians and scholars have misled the average person by referring to ancient civilization as Shemitic, realizing fully that common knowledge of the word "Shemitic" would indicate the language or culture of the Hebrews or Jews only. These scholars knew beyond a doubt that the other two sons of Noah founded civilization and promoted the culture and language of their father, Noah. In fact, Noah's "black" son, Ham, and his generations founded more of the early civilizations than the other two sons.

Please be advised, dear reader, that my labor with the origin of the word "Shemitic" has been to give light where this word has been placed in darkness by what appears to me to be prejudiced scholars who, over the years, have conspired to exclude the culture and contribution of blacks (Hamites) from recorded history.

This is a case in point and a good example of the fact that people other than Israelites spoke the Ashemitic language in the tongue (Amharic) spoken by the Ethiopians, which is today classified as a Shemitic language. This example also proves that Ham, the forefather of the black race, spoke the Shemitic language inasmuch as Cush, the son of Ham, and the father of the nation of Ethiopia is responsible for the Shemitic language of his descendants, the Ethiopians.

While I am extracting light out of darkness, I think it is noteworthy to maintain that during the periods up to A.D., there was no such thing as skin-color prejudices. The Hamites, Japhites, and Shemites interacted and intermarried without regard to the color of the person. For this reason, it was nearly impossible to identify the Hamites and Shemites (Jews) because both groups were dark-skinned and spoke the language of Noah (Shemitic). They were the majority and the dominant group. Much of the early leadership, however, was that of the Hamites. They were the builders of the early civilizations such as Egypt, Ethiopia, Babylon, and Phoenicia.

In the continuation of the likeness and difference of appearance of the early races, it is true that in time, the Japhites isolated or segregated themselves to the north, in what is now called Europe, and intermarried among themselves. They became lighter and lighter in complexion and were easily distinguished from families of the other brothers, Ham and Shem, or if you wish, "races." I wish to make it clear that even though the Japhites were somewhat segregated in Europe from their brothers' children and were lighter in complexion, even during the Greek and Roman civilizations, there was no such idea as color prejudice. Well, if this is so, when and where did color prejudice come from?

9

The source from which color prejudices came are is the United States of America, and it was spread abroad. I will not go into the details of why and when color prejudice started in the U.S.A. at this time because there is another chapter of which I hope to deal with later entitled "The Root of Color Prejudices."

Summary

Now back to the Ethiopian religion and language, which gives one much of the culture of a people. Forty percent of the people belong to the Orthodox Christian Church. About twenty percent are of the Beta Israeli faith, a form of ancient Judaism. They are sometimes called black Jews because they are from Cush, the son of Ham, and thus they have dark skin. They also speak a Shemitic language of the same classification as that of King Solomon of the Bible. According to the U.S.A.'s classification of race, the Ethiopians are black.

Mother Africa

That what is, has not just begun
Because there is nothing new under the sun.
It is from her body all civilizations have sprung.
Yes, Africa is the mother of all nations, the old
and the young.
Be they in Asia, Australia, the Americas or
Europe, from her
civilizations they all have come.
All civilized nations should give praise to
Mother Africa
For the good she has done
For it was she who gave the world science
and math when
it was rather dumb.
It was she who gave the world
medicine, thus disease we
succumbed.
To deny her contributions, is as
promoting the hand without
recognizing the importance of the
thumb.
The world must know it was her
daughter, Egypt, who
fed the children of God (Israel) when
they had not a crumb.
The world must know that it was she
who lived in splendor
when much of the world was near
slums.

In music she gave string instruments
as well as the mighty
drum.
The alphabets came to us from the
Phoenician and Egyptian
sons,
Ship building and navigation from her
children were spun.
The four basic institutions, family,
religion, education, and
government, came from Africa,
civilization's mom.

Chapter 4

The Sons of Ham

According to Genesis 10:6, Ham fathered four sons: Cush, Mizraim, Phut, and Canaan. The Hamites, as referred to in the Bible, were people who would be classified as black in the United States of America today.

Cush (Ethiopia)

Cush (Kush, Hebrew) was the oldest son of Ham, the black son of Noah. Cush was the progenitor of the Ethiopian people. The words "Ethiopia" (Genesis 2:13) and "Cush" (Genesis 10:6) are used interchangeably in scripture. The word "Cush" is a Hebrew word meaning black. "Ethiopia" is a Greek word meaning "burned or black face." "Cush," "Cushan," "Cushi," and "Chushanrishathaim" are all of the same or relative import, especially the word "Cushanrishathaim" which signifies Ethiopian blackness (J. Priest).

On this very account, the ancient country of Ethiopia, then situated in southwest Africa and Asia in the area known as India and Saudia Arabia, as well as the region along the Nile River south of Egypt, was settled first by the family of Cush, called Cushan. Ethiopia, or the country of the dark or black people, was also settled by the family of Cush. Thus, the meaning of the word "Ethiopia," which is a Hebrew word, signifies blackness, a name given to the ancient country on account of the color of its first inhabitants. Please note that I have given the early history of Ethiopia (B.C.).

Ethiopia today is much smaller in land area as well as population, inasmuch as now its boundaries are confined to the continent of Africa. Let us remember, however, that this was not so in the ancient years. I repeat this because of its importance in the understanding of the wealth of contribution made to the world and present civilization by the Cushans who, by U.S.A. classifications, would be called black.

The Cushans once inhabited all of Africa south of the Sahara Desert and that part of Asia now called Saudi Arabia and India. According to the *World Book Encyclopedia*, 1989 edition, vol. 6, p. 376, it was a country located in northeastern Africa. It borders the Red Sea in the north and extends far into the interior of Africa in the south and west. This country's Red Sea coast ranks among the hottest places in the world. Droughts have occurred in Ethiopia from time to time. In the 1970s and 1980s, droughts helped cause severe famines, which led to a large number of deaths.

Ethiopia is one of the oldest African nations. According to the tradition, the first emperor of Ethiopia, Meneliki, was the son of the biblical Sheba and King Solomon of Israel (1 Kings 1:13). Many years later, Ethiopian rulers claimed descent from Solomon and Sheba. Emperors of kings ruled Ethiopia for about 2,000 years.

Early Ethiopian History

Some of the oldest fossil fragments of human beings have been found in Ethiopia. They date from about two million years ago. By 4000 B.C., the blacks of Ethiopia were involved as farmers, shepherds, and traders on a national scale.

The Aksum Kingdom was the first important state after A.D. in what is now Ethiopia. It was well established around A.D. 200, and its capital was in the city of Aksum. The Aksum Kingdom gained much wealth through trade with Arabia, Egypt, Greece, India, Persia, and Rome. Note that Greece and Rome are European white nations many miles from Ethiopia that exported gold, ivory, and spices.

Aksum reached its height of power around A.D. 300 under King Ezana. It is well to note here that the blacks of Ethiopia held religion central to their culture. King Ezana made Christianity the official religion of Aksum. By the way, many of the nations of Europe during 300 B.C. were practicing pagan religion.

My point of note here is that Christianity is not just a white man's religion as some contemporary groups are saying. The Ethiopians lost control of Arabia around A.D. 600, which was years before the discovery of America by Europeans.

Mizraim

Mizraim, the second son of Ham (a black man), was the founder of Egypt, located in North Africa. Egypt is one of the oldest nations in the world. The word "Mizraim" is translated in the revised standard version of the Bible as "Egypt."

The Egyptians were the first people of Egypt. Herodotus, as well as Josephus, says that Menes was the first king and the man who built Memphis, Egypt. They found that most of the inhabitants of this city were black. I was told by Egyptians that Sadat, the late president of Egypt, had a black mother from Memphis, Egypt.

Josephus, the historian, said that when Menes came with his company to the valley of the Nile in Africa, the whole country was one big bog, except a place where Thebes was built, which was on higher ground. The reason for this bog was because every year, the Nile River overflowed the whole valley of Egypt, which extends in length some hundreds of miles and, on average, is about fifty miles wide. The reason for this bog was, according to Herodotus, the water from the Great Flood had not been drained off by ditches and canals, but it was drained afterwards by the first settlers of the Egyptians (black people).

Herodotus also said the Egyptians maintained that they were the most ancient people of the human race and that from them the Greeks borrowed their knowledge of the gods (*Herodotus*, vol. 1, book 2, p. 73, 175, 184).

According to Josephus, Mizraim was the first king and founder of Egypt and second son of Ham. Respecting the Egyptians, Herodotus says Hercules was one of their gods and the second only to Pan (the creator) himself. The Greeks borrowed the knowledge of God from the Egyptians (*Herodotus*, vol. 1, book 2, p. 204).

Hercules/Nimrod

Now who was Hercules? Herodotus stated that Hercules might have been an Egyptian, and his research claims that the god Hercules was the same. Please note that it was Nimrod's leadership that build the Tower of Babel. Also note that the Greek historian learned all of this from the Egyptians, inasmuch as he knew nothing of the story of the Hebrew history, as written by Moses, since that work was translated into the Grecian language not until one hundred fifty years or so after the time of Herodotus.

Who was Nimrod? He was the leader and hero of Babel. He was the greatest type of all the Herculeses of the ancient nations, for the legends of every country who claimed him to be a god represented him as always being armed with a club of enormous size with which he slew the monsters of the earth, dreadful serpents, and wild beasts. In Genesis 10:8–9, it is written that he (the black man) was a mighty hunter before God. The Jewish rabbis interpreted this because of his slaying of wild beasts, which at that time were many in the country of the Euphrates River, where he lived before Cush, his father, and Ham, his grandfather, went to Africa, Ethiopia, and Egypt. Cush and his father founded Ethiopia and Mizraim; his uncle founded Egypt.

Why did Herodotus, the Greek historian, have so much interest in the god Hercules? To find out the true origin of the god Hercules, Herodotus made a voyage from his country, which was on the northeastern side of the Mediterranean near Italy to the city of Tyre, which was on the extreme eastern end of the Mediterranean, the capital of old Phoenicia or old Canaan (country of blacks). The reason he took so much pain on the subject was to see whether his countrymen were right in their claim of Hercules to be their own natural god and not derive from some other people.

When he arrived there, he found, in the city of Tyre, a temple dedicated to Hercules. The next thing for him to learn was how long it had been built. He therefore inquired from the priests the age of the temple. They said it had stood there every since the building of the city, which was more than two thousand years.

This would go back in time from the period when Herodotus went to Tyre, which was about 450 B.C., quite up to the era and birth of Nimrod, which was about one hundred twenty years after the flood.

From this fact, Herodotus was convinced that Hercules was truly a Tyrean, or black people's god, who was also the god of the Egyptians, Ethiopians, and Libyans, as well as of ancient Babylon, of which Nimrod was the founder, although it passed to other hands later in time.

Please note that I have said that Nimrod, the grandson of Ham, was black, and after his death he became a black god after manner of the ancient. Herodotus expressed that the Canaanites and Egyptians, who were the same as the Tyrians, Zidonians, Ethiopians, and Libyans, were black and had curling hair (*Herodotus*, vol. 1, book 2, p. 246).

According to Herodotus, when he was in Africa, some men of Cyrene, a city in North Africa in the country of Libya, told him they had been as far into the interior as the temple of Jupiter Ammon that they had conversed with Estarchas, the king of Ammonia, who had told them that the Libyan race was dwelling still further within the interior and west of Ammonia, and as far west as Egypt, they were all black. This historian says that the whole country south of Jupiter Ammon (or "sheep god") was inhabited by blacks.

In summary, concerning Mizraim, the son of Ham, Nimrod, his nephew, and the grandson of Ham, Mizraim was the founder of Egypt, and Nimrod was the founder of Babylon and was later declared to be the god Hercules. They were all of the black race of mankind.

Phut (Libya)

Ham's third son was Phut. His descendants are not named in the Bible. Josephus says that Phut was the founder of Libya and called the inhabitants "Phutiles." Phut and Libya are mentioned in the Bible as follows: Ezekiel 27:10, 30:5, 38:5; Jeremiah 46:9; and Nahum 3:9. In Nahum 3:9, Ethiopia, Egypt, Phut (Libya), and Lubin are listed as allies of Nineveh, which suggest a political and probably ethnic relationship. According to Genesis, Chapter 10, all of the aforementioned nations descended from Ham. The appellation "Libya," originally meant "black" (Reverend W.D. McKissic, Sr., *Beyond Roots in Search of Black in the Bible*, p. 23).

Canaan (Palestine)

Canaan, Ham's youngest son, was perhaps associated with Ham in most Bible students' minds more than his other brothers because of the *curse* of Canaan recorded in Genesis 9:20–26. Please note that if there was a curse, it was on only one son of Ham, not on Ham and all of his descendants as races have claimed.

Canaan was a son of Ham in the genealogical lists in Genesis 9:10. His descendants occupied the land of Canaan, and from him came the name of the country (Genesis 9:18–22, 10:6).

Canaan was one of the names for Palestine, the land of the Canaanites (the land of the blacks). This was before the Israelites. The area of Canaan, according to Egyptian inscription of 1800 B.C., is the coastland between Egypt and Asia Minor (now Syria), Lebanon, and Israel.

Chapter 5

The Phoenicians

In the *Amarna Letter*, C. 1400 B.C., the name is applied to the Phoenician coast. The Phoenicians lived in the region which is now roughly the capital areas of Syria, Lebanon, and Israel. This area lies between the Lebanon Mountains to the east and the Mediterranean Sea to the west.

The Phoenicians were one of the great people of the ancient world. They were great sailors, navigators, and traders. They became famous in history for two major achievements. They were among the first to send out explorers and colonies throughout the Mediterranean Sea area and even to the Strait of Gibraltar and beyond, possibly to the Americas. The Greek alphabet developed from that of the Phoenicians, and the Roman and all western alphabets (our U.S.A. alphabets) have been taken from the Greeks, who acquired theirs from the Phoenicians (the Canaanites, the black descendants of Ham) (*World Book Encyclopedia*, 1989 edition, vol. d. 15, p. 391).

The Spread of Phoenician (Black) Influence

In this work, I hope to have established that Ham, according to the classification of race by the United States of America, was a black man. Therefore, his children and their children would also be of the black race, thus the Canaanite or Phoenicians will be used interchangeably in this work.

There were Phoenician settlements on the island of Cyprus (an island of Europe) even before 1200 B.C. After that date, the Canaanites opened up the entire Mediterranean to their ships and commerce. Blacks established colonies along the southern coast of what is now Spain (a nation of Europe) and the northern coast of

16

Africa, and the Western Mediterranean was a *black lake* before the coming of the Greeks (whites from northern Europe).

Canaanites influenced Western culture (Europe and U.S.A.) through their colony of Carthage. The Great Phoenician colonies in the west were founded by blacks from the city of Tyre (of the Bible) about 1500 B.C. Also during this period, the Phoenicians (blacks) founded colonies in what is now Mexico and South America (*Mysteries of the Ancient America's, Readers Digest Association, Inc.,* 1992, pp. 130-141). This ancient black American civilization was called "Olmec" by an archaeologist, a term derived from the Aztecs, meaning "dweller in the rubber."

Queen Pido was one of the legendary founders of Carthage. Phoenician colonies, including Carthage, resembled the cities of Phoenicia. It may be well to note that many manufacturers, industrial workers, merchants, and sailors lived there.

The city of Tyre seems to have played the main part in the colonizing activity of the Phoenicians. A vivid description of Tyre's far-flung commerce appears in the Old Testament (Ezekiel 27:3-25). When King David of Israel established his royal residence at Jerusalem, he built his palace with stone and cedars from Lebanon (II Samuel 5:11).

The first book of Kings tells that Hiram, King of Tyre, around 900 B.C. was a friend of King David's successor, King Solomon. When King Solomon built his famous temple, he asked King Hiram of Tyre (a black king) for firs and cedars. Solomon built a navy, and King Hiram loaned him certain workers who were ship men and had knowledge of the sea (I Kings 9:27). In return, wine and other agricultural products went to King Hiram of Tyre of Phoenicia. Other biblical references concerning the Canaanites can be found in Judges 1:9-10, Genesis 12:6-24, Joshua 3:10, and Isaiah 19:18 (Merrill C. Tenny, *Pictorial Bible Dictionary,* p. 143).

The term "Phoenicia" is from a Greek word meaning "dark red." I would surmise that the Greeks gave them that name because it was descriptive of the color of the people (*The World Book Encyclopedia,* 1989 edition, P-15, p. 392-93).

Chapter 6

Blacks throughout the World

New Caledonia

New Caledonia is an overseas territory of France (today). It lies near the South Pacific Ocean about one hundred twenty-three miles northeast of Sydney, Australia. The territory consists of one main island called New Caledonia and other islands called the Loyalty Island; the Be'lep Islands, the Isle of Pines, and a few uninhabited islands.

New Caledonia has a population of about 133,000. Melanesians (black or Hamites), are the largest group of people who make up about two-fifths of the population. Europeans, or Japhites, constitute the other races.

In 1774 James Cook, a British navigator, was the first European to discover the main island. It is said that he called it New Caledonia because it resembled Scotland. The Melanesians (blacks) came from New Guinea about 2000 B.C. to the island that Cook called New Caledonia (*World Book Encyclopedia*, vol. 14, 1989 ed., p. 200).

New Guinea

New Guinea is a large tropical island also in the Pacific Ocean, north of Australia. It ranks as the second largest island in the world. Only Finland is larger. New Guinea has an area of about five million square miles. Most of this area has a cool climate. In contrast, the lowlands along the northern and southern coasts are hot and humid (*World Book Encyclopedia*, vol. 14, p. 206).

Most New Guineans are Melanesians (black), a pacific people who have dark skin and black curly hair. The Hamites of New Guinea have been there since 2000 B.C. Until the 1930s, these New Guineans had little contact with the European world; however, in 1526 Jorge de Memeses, a Portuguese, became the first European to visit what is now called New Guinea. It is believed that the Hamites probably migrated thousands of years ago from Africa to what is now called the Asian mainland, then on to the Pacific Island, including what the Europeans called New Guinea (*World Book Encyclopedia*, vol. 14, 1989 ed., pp. 206 and 207).

New Zealand

New Zealand is an island country near the southwest Pacific Ocean. It lies about one thousand miles southwest of Australia. New Zealand belongs to a large island group called Polynesia. The first people to live in what is called New Zealand, according to Europeans, were a dark-skinned people called Maoris. It is believed that they came to New Zealand from Asia by way of the Polynesian Island. They show a mixture of the Hamite and Semitic races inasmuch as their complexions range from dark brown to light tan. Please remember that the Semitic people were the original people; thus their complexions were dark. In time, as they freely mixed with the Hamites, who were in general a shade darker than the Shemite people, they became somewhat darker since the darker genes are dominant. This same principle also applies to the Japhites (whites) who, during the first few hundred years, lived among the Hamites and interacted together without any discrimination.

In other words, the people of color control the physical outcome of the offspring when it comes to complexion and general physical characteristics. This also has much to do with the reason whites, or European Americans, created a system of color discrimination and enacted laws to prevent marriage between blacks and whites. Please note that the European Japhites discovered New Zealand in 1642; however, they did not start to settle in the islands until the late 1700s.

Inasmuch as I stated that the native people of New Zealand went there from the Polynesian Islands and from Africa and Asia, I think it would be only proper and enlightening to give you some history of these islands called Polynesian (meaning "many islands"). These islands are numbered in the thousands and are scattered across the Central Pacific. The Polynesian Islands are one of three main groups of islands founds among the Pacific Islands, also called Oceania.

Some islands in the Pacific, however, do not belong to Oceania. Islands near the mainland of Asia, such as those that make up the nations of Indonesia, Japan, and the Philippines, are considered part of Asia and are a part of American Islands near North America and South America. The Aleutians and the Galpageoa are grouped with those continents. Australia is itself a continent and is not considered part of Oceania. Although the above-mentioned islands are not a part of Oceania by classification, they are located in the Pacific Ocean and ethnically, the native people are closely related and appear to be descendants of the Hamite stock, or by America's definition of race, they would be classed as black or African Pacific Islands, of which I will use interchangeably.

The African Pacific Islands

Oceania has been divided into three main groups: (1) Melanesia, (2) Micronesia, and (3) Polynesia. The word "melanesia" means "black islands." These islands lie in the southwestern Pacific, north and east of the continent Australia. They were given the name by Europeans because most of the people have rather dark or black skin. Some of the largest islands of Oceania, such as New Guinea and New Britain, are in Melanesia. Other islands of note are a chain of islands called the Solomon Islands, New Caledonia Islands, Loyalty Islands, Vantuatu, Fiji, and the Bismarck Archipelago.

The Melanesia group of islands are located closer to the continent of Australia and the country of islands of Indonesia than the other two groups, which are Micronesia and Polynesia. Micronesia and Melanesia are to the northeast, south of Japan. Polynesia is located east of both Melanesia and Micronesia. The northernmost island group is the Midway Islands, located in the North Pacific Ocean, and the southernmost island is the New Zealand, located in the South Pacific Ocean.

"Micronesia" means "small islands," and it has nothing to do with the color of the people as Melanesia does. Why is it so, do you think, the Europeans did not describe the people in the bordering group of island by complexions (black) as they did the Melanesians? Could it be that it was understood by the Europeans that the people on the smaller islands *were also black*? I think logical deduction would demand that the answer is yes. They all were members of the same family, that of the Hamite stock. The largest island in Micronisia is Guam, of which I will give a brief history later. "Polynesia" means "many islands." These islands, numbering in thousands, are scattered across the central Pacific. There was less attention paid to the Polynesia than the other two islands.

Summary

Let us remember that the first Pacific Islander came from Africa by way of Asia several thousand years ago. Their earliest settlements were in Melanesia (black islands) and Micronesia (small islands). People did not reach most of the Polynesian Islands until much later.

For thousands of years, the people throughout the Pacific Islands lived much alike, except for slight differences in language, dress, laws, and religion. This is because they all came from the same family background, that of their father, Ham (the first black man). Life on most islands was simple and relaxed until the 1500s, when the first European Japhites (whites) arrived in the Pacific. By the late 1800s, several European countries and the United States had taken control of these islands, and the relaxed simple life was changed forever.

A brief description of the three island groups follows:

The Melanesians were the first to come to the Pacific. They are the darkest of the three Pacific Island groups. Many of them resemble African blacks. In addition to their darker skin, they have black woolly hair.

The Micronesians are somewhat taller and have somewhat lighter skin than any of the Melanesians. They generally have wavy hair.

The Polynesians are the tallest and have the lightest skin of the races; however, according to the U.S. classification, they are not light enough to be called white. They have straight to wavy hair.

One of the reasons the Polynesians, who are of the Hamite stock, are lighter than the other two groups and have straight and wavy hair is because marriages between these islands and European and Asian settlements have been more common in Polynesia than in the other Pacific Island regions (*World Book Encyclopedia*, vol. 15, 1989 ed., pp. 2–4).

Australia

Australia is the only country that is also a continent. In area it ranks as the largest country and smallest continent. Australia lies between the Indian and South Pacific Oceans. It is about seven thousand miles southwest of the mainland of Asia.

Keep in mind that Australia, mentioned in this work, is the largest land mass in the Pacific Ocean. It is believed by scholars that the Aborigines, the first people to come to Australia, who are black, make up the oldest group of the Pacific Islanders.

Australia and the Aborigines (Hamites)

Please keep in mind that the objective of this work is to labor to trace the descendants of Ham, the first black man, for the purpose of informing the present-day Hamites of their world history and to show where they were and are presently located on the world scene. Also, it will *open the eyes* of the descendants of Japheth (white people) to the oversight on the part of many *white* scholars of today, due to a deliberate conspiracy conceived by Colonial Americans for the purpose of putting to shame and misinforming all people of African (Hamite) descent and persuading the well-meaning white people (Japhites) that Africans were naturally inferior to them. Please be advised that this action was done in order to destroy the will of Africans to compete economically. It is my position, however, that the behavior on the part of those conspirators has nearly ruined the race relation between blacks and whites, not only in the United States of America, but also throughout the world. Because that seed of hate has been spread abroad, almost every place where whites settled, they used this philosophy to injure and destroy the native dark people (Hamites).

My hope is that people who are deceived descendants of Japheth (whites) will first find shame in the evil work of that small group and work with Hamites to dispel that destructive myth of white supremacy, since that myth is an inherited legacy of dishonor to the white race. When this has been accomplished, only then will America reach her potential where a person "*will be judged by the content of his character rather than by the color of his skin*" (Reverend Dr. Martin L. King).

The word "Aboringin" comes from the Latin word "Aborigine," meaning "from the beginning." When spelled with a small "a," the word "Aborigine" refers to any people whose ancestors were the first people to live in a country. Aborigines have dark brown hair that may be straight, wavy, or curly. Their skin color ranges from tan to dark brown to almost black. Most scientists believe the ancestors of today's Aborigines first arrived in Australia at least forty thousand years ago. Most scientists agree they came to Australia from Asia. But what scientists do not tell you can leave you in the dark. According to most scientists, all people everywhere in the world came to where they are from Asia. This is certainly true with all who believe the story of the Great Flood, of which Noah and his family of eight—three sons of whom were Ham (black), Shem (dark colored), and Japheth (white or lighter)—landed after the flood at Mount Arak in what is now called Asia. From Mount Arak in Asia, they all went to various points throughout the world. The Hamites, being the first to leave home, explored the world and established cities, communities, and systems of government. Some settled in Africa, some in Asia, and others from the mainland settled in the Pacific Islands and the continent of Australia, as well as in Japan, of which I will point out later.

Now reader, do you better understand what I had referenced when I said, "What scientists do not tell you can leave you in the dark"? It is the sincere belief of mine that the attitudes of whites are deliberate or they have been deceived by the institution of color racism conceived and born by those conspirators in America of the colonial period and those who perpetrate the philosophy.

Again, I would like to remind you that the Hamites arrived on the continent of Australia about forty thousand years ago, which was before the Japhites arrived. Remember, the Europeans first reached this land around 1788. It is a shame to say, but the truth needs to be told in hopes that it will set us all free. *That truth is that most of the early European settlers considered the Aborigines (Hamites) to be a primitive people, thus this was their land.* They killed all who resisted and of course, this behavior was not just unique to the Europeans who settled in Australia, but in every country where they settled. The truth is that they ruined the Aborigines and the excuse was they were primitive people.

Readers, can you see how much good would have been bestowed upon mankind if the Europeans had learned and expressed the philosophy "Do unto others as you would have them to unto to you" or "Love your neighbor as yourself"? Yes, today they would be loved and respected throughout the world rather than distrusted and disliked by most people of the world.

The question the writer raises follows: Is it too late for the Japhites (whites) to reestablish themselves as trusting friends to mankind? Well, they are yet alive and as long as there is life, there is a chance for light. It is my hope that enough white people of America and the world will recognize the need of *fair play* for all actors on the stage of life and there is a living God who *sits high* and punishes all evil ones who do not believe that all problems made by mankind can be solved by mankind with the help of God. Thus, the problems of racism were started by mankind, spread abroad, and can be solved by mankind.

Now a few words about the traditional culture of the Australian Aborigines. They lived in harmony with their natural environment as most Aborigines throughout the world did before the arrival of the Europeans. They obtained food by hunting and gathering plants.

Another thing of importance, which seems to link all blacks in contrast to many whites, is the strong family tie. To the Aborigines, family relationships were extremely important. All members of a tribe were related. Marriage united two families, not just two people. Most men had only one wife. Men were the directors. They painted on bark and stone and also engraved designs on rock surfaces. Their carved paintings and other drawings are world-famous. The Aborigines also carved figures from wood and stone and painted them. Some wove beautiful bags, baskets, and mats of twine and cord made from bark, root fiber, fir, and human hair. Aborigines also expressed themselves artistically through music, song, and spoken literature.

Religion linked the Aborigines to the land and nature through ancestral beings who, according to Aboriginal beliefs, had created the world a time long ago called the "Dreaming," or "Dreamtime." They believed these beings never died but just merged with nature to live in sacred beliefs and rituals. In this way, the Aborigines could renew their ties with Dreaming. And just think, the early European settlers called these people primitive. There is food for thought here. Do you see their culture as primitive? I trust not. They had music, government, and religion.

For many years, they were treated the same as American blacks and Native Americans (Indians). They were not looked upon by Europeans as real humans, but today, all Aborigines are citizens of Australia. Even so, most of them face daily unofficial discriminations and prejudice like blacks, where Europeans are in power. Thus, they are underprivileged economically, socially, and politically.

The good news is that many Aborigines are striving to regain ownership of their traditional lands taken by the whites. Some groups have regained titles to large areas in the Northern Territory and in South Australia. In 1980 the federal government formed the Aboriginal Development Commission, which consists of Aborigines (*World Book Encyclopedia*, Vol. 1, 2989 ed., pp. 14–15, reference map of Australia).

India

India's two largest ethnic groups are the Indo-Aryans and the Dravidians. The Indo-Aryans are of lighter skin than the Dravidians. The light-skinned Indo-Aryans live in the north of India, and the dark-skinned Dravidians live in the south. It is said by scholars that the ancestors of the Indo-Aryans who invaded India came from central Asia about 1500 B.C. These people were called Aryans. It is said by the same scholars that the Dravidians (the dark Aborigines) were invaded by the Aryans. These Aryans were of the family of Noah's son Japheth (the white man).

Adolph Hitler, the Nazi director who ruled Germany from 1933 to 1945, used the word "Aryan" for the Germans and other people of northern Europe, who were all white. He claimed the Germans were the purest Aryans and were therefore superior to all other people. Hitler used his ideas about Aryans's (whites) supremacy to justify the killing of millions of gypsies, Jews, and other non-Aryans (non-whites).

The Dravidians

Now let us discuss who the Dravidians were. We find that the Dravidians (dark-skinned) were the earliest known inhabitants of India, which is a very large country in South Asia. Please note that the Aryans invaded the Dravidians around 1500 B.C. and the Dravidians can be traced back at least forty-five hundred years, which mean the Dravidians were in India for at least two thousand years before the Aryans's invasion. This also means the Dravidians came there shortly after the destruction of the Tower of Babel, when God baffled the language of the people. The Dravidians were Hamites (blacks), the first people of what is now called India.

Australoids

Australoids, according to *Webster's Seventh New Collegiate Dictionary*, describes the Aborigines (blacks) of Australia or other people of the Pacific Islands whom I have described as Hamites (blacks). Please note that one of the scholars stated the origin of the Dravidians was uncertain; however, in a cross reference, I found the Dravidians were called Australoids. Now my position is the scholars knew the Dravidians, the Hamites of Australia, and the early inhabitants of the Pacific Islands were of the same stock of people. The main objective of the scholars was to cover up the truth in order to keep the world in the dark as relating to the history and culture of the black man (*World Book Encyclopaedia*, vol. 5, 1989 ed., p. 345).

Please remember earlier in this work I mentioned Aborigines of Australia. The Aborigines were a dark-skinned people who were descendants of Australian settlers who migrated from Asia some forty thousand years ago (*World Book Encyclopaedia*, vol. 1, p. 904).

I feel I have labored successfully with the subject of the origin of the Dravidians to show their origin is Hamite (black) and the white scholars intended for the world to believe the origin of Dravidians was unknown.

Southeast Asia

Southeast Asia covers about one and a half million square miles, or 10 percent of the continent. The area has an average of two hundred sixty-six persons per square mile. The region includes a peninsula east of India and south of China and thousands of islands south and east of the peninsula.

Dear reader, I think it is important to note that a part of East Asia is located in what is now India, where I have already pointed out that the earliest inhabitants were of the Hamite stock. By being aware of this fact, one would better understand the likelihood of Hamites migrating into the area southeast of Asia.

Independent nations make up most of Southeast Asia. Five of them are Burma, Kampuchea, Laos, Thailand, and Vietnam. They all lie on the peninsula. Malaysia lies partly on the peninsula and partly on the mainland.

The European Japhites were not in Southeast Asia before 1500 B.C. We know people were there, don't we? Now the questions are as follows: (1) Who are they? (2) Which race stock do they represent?

We have established the Europeans (whites) came to this area around the 1500s, have we not? We have also established earlier that all people this side of the Great Flood of Noah's day are descendants of Japheth (white man), Shem (reddish, dark man, or Jew), or Ham (black man). We have also stated that the first of the sons of Noah who became world explorers and builders of civilization were the children of Ham. So this would indicate that the people in Southeast Asia would be from the *family tree* of Shem or Ham. Since this is true, one might ask, Why could not the earliest settler of this country have been of Shem? This is a good question. I wish to point out to you that the children of Shem were dark in complexion and some of them were as dark as some of the Hamites due to intermarriage of Hamites and Shemites, but generally they were not dark enough for the white scholars to call them black or negroes. The Shemites had a different and special mission and purpose in mind. It was to carry out the word of God or the teachers of divine truth; therefore, they were to remain near the center of the world in order to keep balance among the rest of the world.

Another point is that the Shemites were very good record keepers and if they had gone to this area, there would like be records to document their exploration, such as the biblical record of their land or journey. Now to the bottom line, in view of what has been stated in the elimination process of the three families, we only have one left, and that is the family of Ham (the black man).

As I stated before, in the 1500s, the Europeans went to Southeast Asia; not only did they go there, but they also began taking control of those countries right away. Now, my dear reader, the irony of their white supremacy philosophy is that they killed the men and begot children by the so-called primitives or healthier women. They also introduced the Christian Church to *convert the heathens*, teaching those things of the Bible that would cause them to accept the oppression inflicted upon them. Why did they kill the natives and take control? Because of one word: *economics*, which equals power and control.

The People of Southeast Asia/Negritos

About four hundred eighteen million persons, or 15 percent, of all Asians live in Southeast Asia. Most Southeast Asians are classified as Asians by the geographical race system that is the same as white schools. When I say they are classified as Asians in the geographical race system, I am saying that most of the people of Southeast Asia are nonwhite. The white supremacy philosophy is as follows: "If you are brown, you are accepted and you may stick around;" however, "if you are black, you are not accepted. You may be pushed back." The majority of people of Southeast Asia, like many of the Chinese, have yellowish to brown skin and black hair. It is said that the ancestors of most Southeast Asians came to the region from Central Asia and South China during prehistory and ancient times. This again takes us back to the time of the Tower of Babel, when the language was baffled and they went abroad (Genesis).

Now, my dear readers, I am sure you are wondering why the people of Southeast Asia had yellowish or brown skin. The reason is because the first people of South Asia were Hamites (blacks). I will now give you documentation of my position from the *World Book Encyclopaedia*, vol. 1, 1989 ed., p. 784. Under the heading "The People," it is written, "Today, descendants of original inhabitants live in those remote areas, some are small blacks called Negritos." For thousands of years, you see, people from Northern Asia settled and mixed (had children) with the original people (blacks); thus, the law of mixing of blacks and whites took its natural course. The offspring are of color; thus, today we have a majority of inhabitants who are yellowish to brown. To this day, some who have not mixed are still black, such as the Negritos.

Negritos

Since I have stated previously that the people of Southeast Asia were called Negritos, it is proper to give a little more information about them.

According to *Webster's Seventh New Dictionary*, the word "Negritos" is of Spanish origin, and it means "small blacks." As stated on page 120, "Negritos are people who live in small isolated groups in the Andaman Islands of the Indian Ocean to the Maya Peninsula, the Philippines, Indonesia, New Guinea, and Australia. Like African pigmies, Negritos have dark skin and tight curly brown hair."

Please be advised, my dear readers, that the Negritos who came from the Andaman Islands, as stated by the scholar who wrote the brief history in the *World Book Encyclopaedia*, were not created there. They were first in Africa or in Asia near Africa, and from there they were in India, and then from India to the Andaman Islands in the Indian Ocean.

Blacks (Hamites) in Mexico and Central America, 5000 B.C.

Mesoamerica: Monuments of a vanished civilization. Where did they go? In the 1920s, archaeologists began to refer to a previously unknown Mexican civilization as "Olmec," a term derived from the Aztecs.

The ancient Olmec civilization began to unfold around 1200 B.C. along the Gulf Coast of southern Mexico and came to an inexplicable end some nine hundred years later. The best way to experience the brilliance of the ancient Olmec civilization is to study the remarkable art these dynamic people left behind.

Black People Created the First Major Civilization in the Americas

The construction of huge, immovable objects is one of the hallmarks of a settled people. The Olmecs were a black people who created the first major civilization in the Americas. Perhaps the most intriguing and exotic of all objects that led to the discovery of the Olmecs were the huge stone heads unearthed in Vera Cruz and Tabasco, Mexico.

History of the Discovery of the Olmec Heads and Mayan Civilization

In 1862 a farmer in Vera Cruz stumbled onto the first of the gigantic black heads, which he mistook at first for an overturned kettle because of its smooth surface. Disappointed that it was not a treasure, he explored no further. Some years later, the head came to the attention of a Mexican archaeologist, José Melgaarv Serrano, who in 1869 reported on the find in a scientific journal. As the first published account of any Olmec found from that area of Mexico, this was a landmark step, although the conclusions Melgaary drew were questionable by the white scientist. "As a work of art," he wrote, "it is without exaggeration a magnificent sculpture—but what astonished me was the Ethiopic-type built pyramid-shaped temples as well as some of the most colossal statuary seen in the ancient world."

From about 5000 B.C., a form of maize (corn) was being cultivated in Mesoamerica (Mexico and Central America). By 2000 B.C., farming villages were well established, and the skills of pottery and weaving were being practiced.

The Olmecs's swampland lies on the east coast of what is now called Mexico. The discovery here of artificially raised platforms and a huge helmeted head carved from basalt and erected by the Olmecs between 500 and 100 B.C. demonstrates the power and organization of this black culture.

The raised platforms and drainage work implies the communal mobilization of manpower. From 1200–600 B.C., the Olmecs built a series of ceremonial centers, which implies a religious nature, the greatest of which was La Venta.

The most grandeur of La Venta were the colossal heads of black men the Olmecs set there. They were carved from giant blacks of basalt, sometimes weighing as much as thirty-four tons, which had to be brought from a rock quarry many miles away.

"It reflects that there had undoubtedly been blacks in this country early in time." Due to racism of the period against blacks and other minorities, Melgaary's report stirred little interest at the time. The discovery of a second similar black head several decades later, however, began to focus archeological attention on this neglected area of Mexico.

Tracing of the Olmec Roots

In 1925 Matthew Stirling embarked on his first exploration of southern Mexico, which was then still archeologically, relatively uncharted country—"a hinterland," he called it. It was a land laced by meandering, sluggish rivers—the most important one the Coatzacoalcos, with its many tributaries and lagoons bordered by mangrove forests. Small settlements of Indian farmers were scattered here and there, usually connected by water transportation. The air was hot and humid, and the annual rainfall sometimes reached one hundred inches. The statement that the first great pre-Columbian society should have arisen in this seemingly inhospitable environment is perplexing. As the anthropologist and Olmec scholar Michael pointed out in 1981, Olmec civilization, like that of Egypt of Africa, is "the gift of the river. Both the Nile of Africa and the many rivers of southern Mexico leave behind deep, rich soil after each year's flooding, conferring an invaluable asset on an agricultural people." Here was land that did not have to be cleared before planting and then left to lie out after two seasons use. What had appeared at first glance to be an environment hostile to settlement and growth of a stable society was shown, on examination, to be as if ordained by God to become a cradle of Olmec civilization.

Gradually, beginning in the 1940s, the legacy of the Olmec civilization and its achievements had emerged. Within a six thousand- to seven thousand-square mile area, there are at least four major ceremonial centers that have been excavated; uncounted smaller ones and hundreds of earthen mounds have yet to be explored. Archeologically the Olmec heartland, as this area has come to be called, is still barely touched. The four major sites that have been explored are San Lorenzo, the earliest center with dates ranging from 1200 to around 900 B.C.; Laguna de los Cerros and La Venta, which both date from around 1000 to 600 B.C.; and the Vera Cruz culture, which followed.

In the early 1940s, when Matthew Stirling first published the results of his excavations at Tres Zapotes and La Venta, where he found works of art ranging from huge stone monuments to fragile clay images, he called forth one of the most savagely unforgiving debates in all archeological history with the racist white scientist. Why so? You see, if it were true that it was the black Olmec people who built this great and first civilization in the Americas, this would destroy their position that black people were innately inferior. This would also say that the credit they had given to the Aztec and Maya Indians as being the first Americans would be false, so they fought Stirling.

"The mysterious producers of this class of art," reported Stirling, "have been called the Olmecs, a people whose origin is as yet very little known." Present archeological evidence indicates their culture which, in many respects, reached a high level, is very early and may well be the basic civilization out of which developed such high art centers as those of the Mayan civilization.

At this point in time, racist scientists attacked Stirling's theory and denied the very existence of the ancient black Olmec. Arguing for Stirling's theory that the black Olmecs were the first great civilization in the Americas, however, were Mexican archaeologists such as Alfonso Caso, who had reconstructed the ruins of Nouote Alban, and Miguel Covarrubias, joined by a small band of American scholars. The fact that some pieces had been found—a stele (known as stele C) in Tres Zapotes and a small jade statuette in the shape of a duck with hieroglyphic writing and date that preceded Mayan civilization—was dismissed by the racist white archaeologist.

Thanks be to God, in the mid-1950s, when radio carbon dating of La Venta artifacts proved irrefutable proof of the black Olmec antiquity and importance, the existence of the civilization was widely accepted. At last, recognition as the mother culture of Mesoamerica (Mexico and Central America) as black people became a part of archeological history.

In conclusion, of all the Olmec ceremonial centers, none exceeds La Venta in impressiveness. It has been called "the glory of the ancient Olmec." It stands on an isolated sandy island, two miles square, which rises some forty feet above the surrounding swampland and the tidal Tonal a River. The ceremonial precincts lie roughly in the center of the island and are made up of a sunken plaza and pyramids, including one whose shape is unique in all the New World. Rising some one hundred three feet above the rectangular site, it dominates the other structures. It was built of three and a half million cubic feet of clay. Some scholars have suggested that this pyramid commemorates their ancestral origins. Whatever the inspiration may have been, the pyramid exemplifies wisdom, the sheer mentality of Olmec construction, and the unlimited man hours of backbreaking labor that went into it.

What is true of their building is equally true of their sculpture. The large pieces are characterized by an imposing massiveness. At La Venta, Stirling found four colossal heads (black men) each weighing as much as twenty tons and a giant stele (GK, pillar, inscribed stone slab) that weighted fifty tons and stood fourteen feet tall. Seven altars, one of which measured eleven and a half feet in length and more than five feet high, were also unearthed, rectangular in shape and carved with figures and scenes. These stupendous blocks of stone looked like altars but may actually have been thrones for Olmec rulers.

Since there were no stones suitable for carving in the swamplands around La Venta, they had to be transported from the Tuxla Mountains, which lie fifty-six miles west of the site. How did the Olmec, with primitive technology of the Stone Age (in Europe) move the huge blocks and boulders of basalt, the igneous dark gray to black stone that was used in the sculpture? This is the same question scholars asked of the Egyptian pyramids of Africa. "The logistics of transporting these stones," writes Michael Cole, "compromises one of the great puzzles of New World archeology, and there have been many attempts to solve the problem. At San Lorenzo, for instance, it took fifty workers to lift a head upright using poles and ropes, small efforts compared to the magnitude of the task faced by the Olmec."

I wish to note here that neither brute nor strength nor limitless patience alone could make such a prodigious task possible. They also called for a well-run social machine, an obedient work force, and a strong guiding hand from the seat of power. Anthropologists agree that Olmec society was, in fact, authoritarian and highly stratified. Like the Mayans who followed the Olmec people, the society below the rulers was divided into administrators, engineers, foremen, and straw bosses with a large subservient peasantry at the base.

Please note that three thousand years after the Olmec lived, their colossal heads give us some idea of what these ancient rulers looked like. Among scholars, it is now almost universally accepted that the colossal heads so far have thirteen in all from three different sites and are portraits of Africans or people of African descent who were the first people in what is now Mexico and Central America. The Mayan and the Aztec, of which the American scholars have credited the development of the rich civilization of Mexico and Central America, was built off that of the African Olmec. Please note that this explains why the people of Mexico and Central America are very dark in complexion.

Now I shall labor to show the connection of the Mayan and Aztec to the Olmec.

Mayan Civilization Built from the Olmec (Black) Civilization and Their Relationship to the Olmec

It is very important to understand that when the Europeans first landed on the shores of Mexico's Yucatan Peninsula early in the sixteenth century, the great Mayan centers were already faded relics—time worn, overgrown, and abandoned.

They found deep within the dense tropical forests or clustered on the barren limestone tip of the peninsula not one or two monuments, or even one or two settlements, but vast architectural complexes studded with palaces and pyramids, each structure and each setting a triumph of grace and power.

These sixty or so Mayan "cities" were simply the most visible and enduring evidence of a civilization spectacular in its learning and achievements. In addition to being master engineers and architects, the black Mayans were sophisticated mathematicians and accomplished astronomers like the Olmec before them. They seemed to have refined the complex hieroglyphic system of writing for recording the past, however, and were thus better historians than their predecessor, the Olmec.

It is unfortunate that the true dimensions of Mayan civilization were lost due to the Spaniards who, in their haste to conquer and convert, failed to understand what lay before their *very eyes*.

Note, if you will, that not until the nineteenth century did the extent and grandeur of Mayan culture begin to be fully explored and publicized by Europeans and Americans, awakening a captivated world to the fact that high civilization on the order of ancient Egypt of Africa had flourished for nearly two thousand years in the New World. Be mindful of the fact that at this point in time, the European and American scholars did not know the Olmec existed.

To appreciate the accomplishment of the Mayans as well as their relationship to the Olmecs, one must first understand their geography. The Mayans inhabited the same territory of the earlier people of the Olmec. This territory was some one hundred twenty-five thousand square miles, encompassing the present-day countries of Honduras, El Salvador, Guatemala, and Belize, and the Mexican states of Tabasco and Chippas to the west, as well as the entire Yucatan Peninsula, which is bordered by the Gulf and Caribbean Coasts. Most Mayanists would agree that its roots go back to the Olmec (black) civilization, which flourished on the nearby Gulf of Mexico during the years from 1200 to 300 B.C. ("The Olmec Enigma," pg. 130, *Mysteries of the Ancient Americas*).

The Olmec are thought to have served as the other culture for several Mesoamerican groups; however, the most popular are being discussed in this work: the Mayan, Aztec, and Inca of South America.

An example of the Olmec being the mother culture is they are highly regarded for their particular skills in sculpting monumental stone heads and for their intricate jade carving. They have also been credited with being the first in

Mesoamerica to construct a calendar and a system of hieroglyphics, two intellectual milestones upon which the Mayans later built. A stele (stake or pillar) was found carved in the Olmec style and dated "32 B.C." with the bar and dot strengthening the case of those who credit the intellectual strength of the Mayan culture to an Olmec ancestry.

Let us be reminded that the central objective of this work is to trace the lineage of Ham of the Bible, the progenitor of what has been called the black race of humankind, and to show the contribution to humanity made by the descendents called Hamites. I also stated in the introduction that the names "African," "black," and "Hamite" would be used as the same people. I also feel I should bring to your attention that I said I would use European and American "whites definition" of for those persons in America who are of African descent. That definition states a person is considered black if he has any known African blood or shows any of the physical characteristics of an African. Thus the Olmecs, Aztecs, and Incas are considered Hamites in this work, and those present-day Mexicans are considered to be their descendants. I further wish to say that due to my research, the Olmecs and Mayans are one and the same people. As a comparison, the first thirteen colonies of the U.S.A. were British as far as culture and general ethnicity; however, in time, the behavior of surrounding ethnic groups caused change. But the religion, education, and government remained basically the same to this day; so it is with the Olmec and Mayan civilizations. In the following pages, I shall labor to prove my point of view.

Let us start with the name "Olmec," which does not follow the tradition for naming a person, place, or thing. The question is, why give a name in the first place? The answer to that question is the name is given to describe what the person, place, or thing is—to describe its nature. Now in case of the Olmec people, this is not so. The name "Olmec" means "Land of Ruber of the People of the Land of Ruber," which does not say anything about the people, but the place. The second point to be considered is the fact that both the Olmec and Mayan dwelled in the same general area of Central America and Mexico. The timelines, however, were of course at different periods, to some degree. Thirdly, the Olmec did not name themselves. Others did.

According to scholars, people lived in the area of Central America and Mexico around 5000 B.C., and a form of maize was being cultivated. By 2000 B.C., farming villages were well established, and the skills of pottery and weaving were being practiced. Who the people were, from 5000 B.C. to around 1300 B.C., the scholars are not sure. They do, however, date a high civilization of people from 1200 B.C. to 300 B.C. called the Olmec. Now please note that they date the Mayans A.D. 300 to A.D. 900 as their classic period, which I interpret as the height of their civilization, and from 900 A.D. to 1500 A.D. as their post-classic period, of which I interpret as the decline of the Mayan civilization. Remember that when the Europeans first landed on the shores of Mexico in the sixteenth century, they found the great Mayan centers were already "faded relics timeworn, overgrown, and abandoned" (*The Magnificent Maya Mysteries of the Ancient Americans*). In conclusion, I am saying that the people called Mayan were the Olmec with a mixture of other tribes who had migrated to the area. I shall continue to defend my point of view as I give more evidence that the Olmec and Mayan were basically the same people.

On page 153 of the *Magnificent Maya Mysteries of the Ancient Americans*, we find that the Mayans, in time and chronology, were led to develop their mathematics (which they inherited from the Olmec culture) to such a degree of sophistication that it surpassed that of the Greeks and Romans. Like the Olmecs before them, the Mayans practiced skill deformation. Jade in particular was greatly valued by the Mayans, as it had been uncovered in 1939, further strengthening the case of those who credit the intellectual strength of the Mayan culture to an Olmec ancestry. In other words, evidence on stele inscriptions now made it clear that the Olmec older civilization as a whole lagged behind the Mayan, their children, or neighbors to the south because most of the Olmec in other areas were in a state of decay. These are just a few examples of how the scholars refer to the Olmec.

Mayan Golden Age

The Mayan Golden Age, or Classic Era as it is called by some, lasted about A.D. 300 to A.D. 900, the climax of some six centuries of study, growth, and development. Now, please note, "most Mayanists would agree that its roots go back to the Olmec civilization (black civilization), which flourished on the nearby Gulf of Mexico during the years of roughly 1200 B.C. to 300 B.C." ("The Olmec Enigma," p. 130, *Mysteries of the Ancient Americas*).

Please note, the Olmec are thought to have served as the mother culture for many Mesoamerican groups. The definition of Mesoamericans is they were one of several settled people of that period, descendants of nomads who likely came to the North American continent from Asia after the arrival of the Olmec. It is very important to understand Asia then was not anything like the Asia of the past two thousand or so years. The Asia of 500 to 1000 B.C. was a culture of Hamites (blacks) with a mixture of Japhites. Please note that boundaries and names of countries as we know them today were given by Europeans (Japheth) after they gained power some time in B.C. under the philosophy of "claim it and name it." In other words, it was long before the Mayans, who were mixtures of some nameless bands of people possessing varied cultures and speaking a variety of languages.

Hamites (Blacks) Built First Calendar in America

Probably no other people except perhaps the ancient Egyptians and Babylonians, who were Hamites, have been more preoccupied with time as the Mayans. They plotted the movement of the planets, sun, and moon with remarkable accuracy, often timing wars and other important events of their lives according to celestial cycles.

These are examples, perhaps by observation with the naked eye (I say perhaps because we don't know what instruments they may have had). Careful notations over hundreds of years, unknown generations of patient Mayan and Olmec astronomers before them, worked out a complex series of calendars, including the cycle of the moon and sequences of 260, 365, and 360 days. They had a 360-day year, which was made up of eighteen months of twenty days each. It was used in a

32

system call the "Long Count," which recorded the exact number of days elapsed since a zero date, corresponding to August 13, 3114 B.C. The 260-day was the religious year calendar (Yes, they were religious) consisting of twenty months of thirteen days each. It was linked to the 365-day solar calendar by means of the "Calendar Round" scale, which spanned fifty-two solar years or seventy-three religious years, so that any day could be identified in both cycles at the same time. Just think for a minute, all of this Hamite intellectualism has been kept from the general public educational system and especially from the descendants of Ham, the black people of the world.

Example of "Holocaust" and "Genocide" of a Primitive Hamite People, the Tasmanian and Flinders by Modern Japhites (Whites)

I shall begin this chapter by giving the location of the Tasmania and Flinders and secondly, a brief description of their culture and the period in which they lived. Thirdly, I will show their demise by the Europeans, which is the holocaust and genocide.

Location

The Tasmania and Flinders Islands are located about one hundred fifty miles south of the continent of Australia. The Flinders Island and Tasmania Island are separated by a fourteen-mile strait of water, the larger of the two islands in Tasmania over twenty-six thousand square miles in area, about the size of Ireland. It is believed that these islands are severed pieces of the Australian continent. Much of the east is dry eucalyptus forest; the west, very wet rain forest; and the core, rugged mountains, covered in the winter with snow. All those ecological zones and the food resources these islands offer can be found in Australia just one hundred fifty miles to the north.

About the People of Tasmania and Flinder

When Tasmania was discovered by Europeans in 1642, it was inhabited by around five thousand Hamites who were similar in appearance to the Hamites of the Australian mainland. Their hair and skin were very dark. They had deep-set eyes, their noses were broad, their mouthes were wide, their lips were full, their cheekbones were prominent, their build was lean, and their limbs were long and slender. The Tasmanians differ from the mainlanders of Australia, however, principally by having woolly rather than straight or wavy hair. It is said that Tasmanians's latitude is that of Chicago, which causes the country to be rather cold in winter.

What is amazing about the Tasmanians is they did not use heat in their huts and virtually went naked, winter and summer. Granted they were probably better adapted metabolically to withstanding cold than are most. Such metabolic adaptations have been demonstrated by the Hamites of Tierra del Fuego Indians on the southernmost tip of South America, who similarly went naked in cold environments. If

33

you recall in the chapter about the Olmec (the first people of Mexico, Central, and South America who were black or Hamites), you should better understand the reason the Tierra del Fuego Indians went naked. They were the same people. By the way, "Tierra del Fuego" is from the Spanish language, translated into English, meaning "Land of Fire." Since it was cold there and they went naked, could this be an incorrect translation? Perhaps the correct translation of "Tierra," which means "land and del, of, and Fuego, fire," would be land without fire, and the word "sin" means "without food for thought." Although they did not wear clothes for protection from the cold, they smeared themselves with a mixture of animal fat, charcoal, and ocher. Ocher is an earthy impure iron ore used by the Tasmanians as a pigment-based ointment.

Please note that the tribes in the mild climate of east Tasmania did not have houses to shelter themselves against wind and rain; they just had windbreakers of bark and branches. Tasmanians used stone tools such as flaked scrapers to make a few types of wooden tool, which were roughly shaped and held in the hand. Those wooden tools in turn consisted of spears, clubs that were also thrown as projectiles, and sticks used to dig up roots or pry up shellfish. They wove plant fibers into baskets and made ropes for tree climbing. They also made water buckets from kelp fronds and pouches from animal skins. Their art and decoration were restricted to necklaces of shells or other materials: rock carvings or stencils, decorative scars, ocher rubbed on the hair, and charcoal rubbed on the skin.

Their mode of transportation was a type of watercraft, which is important for understanding how the Tasmanians could have gotten from Australia to Tasmania across the one hundred fifty-mile gap of Bass Strait. These boats were rafts with a gentle depression, like a flattened canoe, and were made of bundles of rushes or bark strips that floated because of their own buoyancy and trapped bubbles. A more advanced type of boat is used to this day in that part of the world.

Some features of Tasmania technology were shared with mainland Hamites (aboriginal) Australians, who also lacked agriculture, metal, pottery, and bows and arrows. The aboriginal in English is defined as an adjective, denoting the first, original, or native from the beginning, thus I wish to remind you that these Hamites were the first people in these lands. This in fact was their country, and to this day the continent of Australia and the islands there are still theirs. Tasmanians lacked many things, however, their mainland brothers and sisters of the Australian mainland had, such as the boomerang, spear thrower (a hand-held device to increase a spear throwing distance and propulsive force), ground or polished stone tools, mounted stone tools (hatchets or adzes with a handle, a cutting tool different from an axe in having an arching blade set at right angles to the handle), bone tools (needles and awls, a pointed instrument for piercing small holes as in leather and wood), fire-making equipment (fire drill), nets, traps, or hooks to catch fish, birds, or mammals. Without mounted tools, Tasmanians could not fall a big tree, hollow out a canoe, or carve a wooden bowl. Without bone tools, they could not sew warm clothes or make watertight bark canoes.

With knowledge of the Tasmania material culture, one can see how easy it was for the Europeans (Japhites) with guns and other superior weapons to take over their land and destroy the people, which will be noted later in this work. I will also show how cruel and malicious they were.

How Did the Tasmanians Reach Tasmania from Australia, Which was Separated by the Bass Strait, One Hundred and Fifty Miles Wide?

This mystery is solved by realizing that during the Pleistocene Ice Ages, when much of the world's water was locked up in glaciers, sea level was more than four hundred feet below its present level. The Pleistocene Ice Age is the earlier epoch of the Quaternary or the corresponding system of rocks (*Webster's Seventh New Collegiate Dictionary*). The Ice Age was a time of widespread ice glaciations.

As a result, shallow straits like the Bass Strait were then dry land connecting the land masses they presently separate. This, Ice Age Tasmania was not an island, but the southeast corner of Australia. Calculations of past sea level fluctuations estimate that the Bass Strait was dry land before 55,000 years ago, then water from 55,000 to about 37,000 years ago, and intermittently or continuously dry again from about 37,000 to 10,000 years ago, after which glacial melting drowned the land bridge and finally restored Tasmania's form to the island we know today.

Thus, the answer to the question of how the Tasmanians colonized Tasmania despite their inability to cross Bass Strait is simple. They were Hamite Australians who walked to Tasmania when it was a part of Australia. The oldest known human site in Tasmania has been radio-carbon dated at about 35,000 years. That date implies that black people crossed from Australia to Tasmania soon after the land bridge reemerged around 37,000 years ago. The rising seas eventually drowned the Bass Strait, thus closing the trap on them, commencing their long isolation.

In a border context, the above illustration is important for our understanding of how the Hamites, the first world explorers, proceeded not only from Australia to Tasmania, but to the rest of the world as well. Look at a map, and you will see that North Australia is separated from New Guinea by less than one hundred miles and from the island of Indonesia by less than two hundred miles, of which I have discussed earlier in this work. All of the first people were black or Hamites. Indonesia and New Guinea had big sailing vessels capable of covering those distances in a few days or less. Indonesian fishermen have been visiting North Australia for many centuries. In that time, there was also regular trade between South New Guinea and Northeast Australia along the chain of islands between them. Many inventions and possessions, besides just tools and animals, must have entered Australia by these routes.

This type of trade and diffusion of inventions converted by Hamites or blacks has had major influences on human history. To name two examples, domesticated plants and animals spread back and forth from Africa to Middle East to Europe. The wheel, probably invented by Hamites around five thousand years ago in what today we call the Middle East, or Black Sea area, spread rapidly westward across Europe. All other things being equal technology developed more slowly in isolated societies than in highly connected societies because the latter have access to many other people's inventions besides their own. Remember, however, Tasmania was cut off from all outside input ten thousand years before the Europeans discovered them in the seventeenth century, and the only inventions available were those of the Tasmanians themselves. Thus, the British (Japhites) were able to easily invade and obliterate the black Hamites, and they killed all of them but one woman, who reported the story of what happened to her people.

The Holocaust and a Primitive People

The Tasmanians' ten thousand years of isolation came to an end on December 2, 1642, when the Dutch skipper Abel Tasman landed on what was later named for him, Tasmania. The second European visit was by the Frenchman Nicholas Marion du Fresne, who landed on March 4, 1772. It is recorded that within a few hours, his sailors had shot and killed several defenseless Tasmanians. European (Japhites/whites) occupation of Tasmania began with the arrival of seal hunters in the mid-1790s and of British soldiers and sailors in 1803. The record shows the British used cannons to massacre thousands of Tasmanians on May 3, 1804. Those whites treated the Tasmanians very cruelly, kidnapping Tasmanian women and children and often killing the women's husbands or the children's parents in the process. Some of them kept between two and five Tasmanian women each for sex and slave labor, sometimes keeping them tied and shooting them if they did not work well or tried to escape. The whites were especially dependent on these black women, since the women could dive for shellfish and were good at killing seals. As one example of the kidnappings and killings, a northeast Tasmanian tribe was reduced to seventy-two adult men, three adult women, and no children. What made this even worse was no Europeans were ever punished for murdering Tasmanians, and only a few Europeans were punished for mistreatment. For example, they received twenty-five lashes for tying Tasmanian women to logs and burning them with firebrands or forcing a woman to wear the head of her freshly murdered husband on a string around her neck.

When Turkish settlers poured into Tasmania in the 1820s, after the Napoleonic Wars, racial conflict intensified. The whites regarded Tasmanians as little more than animals and treated these black people accordingly. Tactics for hunting these people of color included riding out on horseback to shoot them, setting out steel traps to catch them, and putting out poison flour where they might find and eat it. In some cases, they cut off the penises and testicles of some of the Hamite men to watch them run a few yards before dying. It is said that at a hill christened Mount Victory, whites slaughtered thirty Tasmanians and threw their bodies over a cliff. It is recorded that one party of white men killed seventy Tasmanians and bashed out the children's brains.

In 1828 the European governor of Tasmania declared martial law, permitting Europeans to shoot on sight any aborigine found in European-settled areas. This was followed by roving search-and-capture parties (five convicts of good character led by a field police constable) and by a bounty established in 1830 of five pounds per Tasmania adult and two pounds per child. Finally, the British Christian Church became involved. A missionary, George Augustus Robinson, was hired for the price of one thousand pounds to round up the remaining blacks of Tasmania and remove them from Tasmania. In 1830 he could find only three hundred people of color on the island of Tasmania out of the original estimated population of five thousand. The next to the last group numbering eight was captured in 1834, but a further group of about six remained at large until 1842 (the last original people of color of Tasmania).

It is sad to write the final outcome of these Hamites; however, the story must be published as a warning that this type of thinking is still alive among some people.

Most of the Tasmanians died in the course of the roundup. Robinson, the Christian missionary, however, collected approximately one hundred thirty-five survivors and brought them to a windy site with little fresh water at Wybalenna on the Flinders Island, of all places, the Tasmania Isle of the Dead. Of course, most of these blacks died there, sick and brokenhearted. Forty-seven came back to Tasmania in 1847; there the last one, a woman name Truganini, died in 1876. With Truganini's death, it appeared that white settlers had reached a final solution for their problems of race relations, by exterminating these helpless people of color.

I wish to note that left behind were many children born to these black women and white men. They segregated their children, their descendants, by placing them on the Furneaux Islands, a reserve where their descendants were until recently forbidden by the government to leave.

Commentary

During the twentieth century, the number of people of black and white Tasmania descent is estimated to be around four thousand, though it could be considerably higher because racial prejudices make people reluctant to be identified as aboriginal Tasmanians.

The new and present Tasmania government policy is the same as the white American's of 1995 and 1996 concerning affirmative action for white women and people of color, which is that *all Tasmanians should be treated equally*. What this means is that disadvantaged blacks, Tasmanians, should get no special help. The white government of Tasmania denies the existence of Tasmanians of color and their problems, and it also denies any continuity between the original Tasmania culture and the descendants' lives today. It also denies any connection of the descendants to their land and hopes they will soon assimilate and eventually the social problem of injustices to the people of color will go away at no cost to the descendants who reaped riches at their demise. The common view is like that of the U.S.A. of the 1900s: the Tasmanians of color receive government grants unavailable to whites.

Jose Maria Morelos Y Pavon
Biography of a Mexican of African Descent
Who Was a Commander in the War of Independence

The great commander in the War of Independence of Mexico was born in the city of Valladolid in 1765. This city is now called Morelia in his honor. His parents were of humble extraction, and Morelos was a farmer up to the age of twenty-five. Due to his great dedication, ambition, and doing without, in 1791 he was admitted to the San Nicolás School, which was located in the same city where he was born. The principal of that school was Miguel Hidalgo. Morelos became a priest in 1796, and the towns of Carácuaro and Nocupétaro became his ministry. He lived in the first town, and because of this fact, he was later known as "the Priest of Carácuaro."

When Hidalgo declared war, Morelos offered his services to him. As a colonel, he was in charge of raising the rebellion in the south of the country. His repeated victories forced brigadier Callaja to lead a numerous army against him. Morelos took post in Cuauta, resisting bravely for two months until he broke the blockage on May 2, 1812, which gave him recognition as a man of war. His repeated victories brought about the conquest of Daxaca and Aculco (1813).

The National Congress met in Chilpancingo on September 13, 1813, and declared the independence of the country, and Morelos was given executive power. Morelos accepted it, provided that his title would be "Servant of the Nation" and not "Your Highness," which was the title people wanted to give him. Besides his military functions, Morelos was in charge of executing the decisions of the Congress and being under its protection. On December 23, 1813, Morelos attacked Valladolid with the biggest army he ever had under his command. Valladolid was defended by Llano and Iturbide with great courage. On the night of the December 24, 1813, there was a lot of confusion and Morelos's soldiers attacked each other, causing a lot of casualties, which was made worse by the defeat of Puruapán (January 5, 1814).

The realists did not stop pursuing Morelos, who had the big task of guarding the Congress and the government. He was forced to constantly move from one place to another, and this made his military operations very complicated. On November 5, 1815, while he was protecting the Congress on its way to Tûhacán, Morelos was forced to combat in Tezmalaca, where he was defeated by the realists, commanded by Colonel Concha. Morelos was taken prisoner. He was sentenced to death in Mexico City.

Reference

Author. *Herodotus*, Vol. 1, Book 2. 73, 175, 87. City: Publisher, Year.

Author. "The Olmec Enigma." *Webster's Seventh New Collegiate Dictionary/Mysteries of the Ancient Americas*, 130. City: Publisher, Year.

Author. *Encyclopedia Deconocimentos El Nuevo Tesoro De La Juventud, Tomo XII*, 41, 211, 212. City: Publisher, 1983.

Flavius, Josephus. *Antiouties of the Jews, Book 1*, 12. City: Publisher, Year.

Leo, John. *History of Ancient Africa in the Arabic Language, Uni Feo*, Vol. 2. 754-781. City: Publisher, Year.

McKissic, Sr., Rev. W.A. *Beyond Roots in Search of Blacks in the Bible*, 23. City: Publisher, Year.

Readers Digest Association. *Mysteries of the Ancient Americas*, 130-141. City: Publisher, 1992.

Russell LLd, Rev. Michael. *View of Ancient and Modern Egypt, Palestine of the Holy Land*, 257. City: Lawrence Lectures, Year.

Shaw, Dr. Thomas. *Procopius, A Greek Historian of the Sixth Century*, Page Numbers. City: Publisher, Year.

Shaw, Dr. Thomas and Procopius. *The Universal Traveler*, 467. City: Publisher, Year.

Tenny, Merrill C., ed. *Pictorial Bible Dictionary*, 143. City: Publisher, Year.

World Book Encyclopaedia Vol. 6. 376. City: Publisher, 1989.

Pamphlets and Spoual Sources

American Antislavery Society, Annual Report. New York 1934-39. The Annals, American Academy of Political and Social Science, March, 1956. Entire volume directed to "Race Desegregation and Integration" edited by Lia De A. Reid, National Association for the Advancement of Colored People Annual Report. New York, 1911-1981.

The Roots of Color Prejudices

The roots of color prejudices cannot be understood if they are not placed in the flow of history by which they will appear that slavery is not a disgrace peculiar to blacks but a world phenomenon that has been practiced for centuries. Men—black, brown, and white—have been bought and sold.

There was, however, a great difference between ancient slavery and modern slavery. Ancient slavery had nothing to do with color or race. It was primarily a part of the rules of war.

Let us note that in the sixteenth century, when America was a wilderness, much of Europe had been reduced to beggary. Benin, a city of Africa, was a prosperous place twenty-five miles wide with large boulevards and intersecting streets flanked with houses and verandas.

Impressed by these and other evidences of African power, the first European emissaries greeted Africans as allies and partners in trade. The letters and diaries of trade show that down to the eighteenth century, they had no conception of Africans as inferior, nor did they show any state of white supremacy or color prejudices. On the contrary, many of these traders said that Africans were their equals and superior to many of their countrymen.

Africans were of the same mind. They did not consider themselves inferior to Europeans. If anything they considered themselves superior to the odd-looking men with pale skins. It is said that the King of Dahomey, an African, seldom shook hands with white men.

I wish to note that during this period, both Africans and Europeans profited in trade and commerce. Also, some young men of the ruling class went to Lisbon and Rome to study and observe. Black and white kings exchanged letters filled with terms of royal endearment. They also exchanged gifts and mistresses of various hues. On May 15, 1518, one hundred years before the Jamestown landing, Henry of the Congo, Africa, led a mission to the Vatican, Rome, formally addressed the

40

Pope in Latin, and was appointed Bishop of the Congo. In Rome, Lisbon, and other European centers, Africans rose to high positions in church and state.

Again, I point out that to this point in time, there were no color prejudices in the culture of white people. There was commingling of peoples from different lands and cultures.

Well, now, the question on the floor is, what happened to cause the change of white thinking and attitude from color blindness to color prejudice? As the story goes, this is what happened. While the bright young black men were feasting in the courts of Lisbon and while the black priests were involved in the courts of the Vatican, events were happening in the outer world that would destroy this relationship between blacks and whites and change Europe and Africa forever.

The cause of whites to start thinking color prejudice began with the Europeans' discovery of America and the opening New World. It is interesting to note that descendants of the first black captives—black Christians born in Spain and Portugal—were with the first European explorers and settlers. Black explorers, servants, slaves, and free men accompanied Spanish and Portuguese explorers in their expeditions in North and South America. Consequently the root cause of whites to think color prejudice was economic, not race-related.

To understand this fact in its fullness, we have to notice first that the rulers of the colonies were not overly concerned about the color or national origin of the workforce. They tried Indian slavery, and they also tried to enslave white men and women. When the attempt failed, the spotlight fell on Africans. The explanation is to be found in the situation that defined Africans, Europeans, and Indians. Whites were under the protection of recognized governments; they could appeal to a monarch or to white opinion. Whites, being "white," could escape and blend into the crowd. Indians, too, could escape; they knew the country, thus they could go back home. The white rulers of the colonies said and apparently believed that Indians tended to sicken and die under slavery conditions.

Africans did not have these disadvantages. The Spanish said they were strong. One African was worth four whites or Indians. They were inexpensive; the same money that would buy an Irish or Englishman for seven years would buy an African for life. They were visible and they could run, but they could not blend into the white crowd. Also, they were unprotected.

In the sixties of the seventeenth century, the men who ran the colonies, egged on by the slave-trading royalists of London, made a decision that would lead to black color prejudices. That decision continues to this present age.

Yes, men decided to base the American economic system on black human slavery organized around the distribution of color in human skin. Virginia and Maryland led the way, enacting laws in the 1660s that forbade intermarriage and made blacks slaves for life. The idea was adopted with minor modifications by other colonies. After this, White America found it necessary to create an ideology of racism that justified the subordination of blacks and the destruction of the established bonds of community between blacks and white servants, who constituted the majority of the population.

In conclusion, on the roots of color prejudices, the last questions on the floor are: Who were these persons who created color prejudices, and why?

They were the "good white people"—Christian planters, preachers, lawyers, and aristocrats—thus the "founding fathers" the government.

Why did these "good church-going people" do this devilishness to Africans? Yes, for economics, money.

Yes, whites and blacks once lived together as equals, and it will happen again with the proper education in true history of what caused the great divide.